£4.60

al & Bute

4.
5.
6.
7. ... & Iona
8. ... Galloway   24. Orkney
9. D... & Galloway   25. Orkney in Wartime
10. Dundee & Angus   26. The Outer Hebrides
11. Edinburgh   27. The City of Perth
12. Fife, Kinross & Clackmannan   28. Highland Perthshire
13. Glasgow   29. Ross & Cromarty
14. Inverness   30. Royal Deeside
15. Islay, Jura, Colonsay & Oronsay   31. Shetland
16. The Isle of Skye   32. Stirling & The Trossachs

The remaining four books, Caledonia, Distinguished Distilleries,
Scotland's Mountains and Scotland's Wildlife feature locations
throughout the country so are not included in the above list.

PICTURING SCOTLAND

ARGYLL

COLIN NUTT
Author and photographer

2   The very south of Argyll: the magnificent sweep of Brunerican and Dunaverty Bays on the southern shore of Kintyre, taken from the road that leads to the Mull of Kintyre. Towards the right of the

ARGYLL

...icture is Dunaverty Head (see p.10) and the headland in the middle of the picture is Keil Point.   **3**

Welcome to Argyll!

In total, the magnificent realm of land and water that is Argyll stretches approximately 120 miles up Scotland's western seaboard, incorporates 26 inhabited islands and is a hotbed of ancient history. Its many sea lochs and islands make Argyll's coastline longer than that of France; its landmass of 6,930 sq. km. makes it larger than Belgium. Due to its size and range, this book will concentrate on Argyll's mainland, taking in districts such as the Kintyre Peninsula, Knapdale, Kilmartin, Oban, Loch Fyne, Benderloch, Appin and Glen Orchy. Within these territories are all the shades of scenery and as many aspects of mankind's influence upon it as anyone could wish to find. Its geographical range encompasses some of Scotland's highest mountains, its longest inland loch and a coastline that is in part reminiscent of the Mediterranean and at times battered and shaped by the ferocity of the Atlantic storms that frequently assail it.

The name 'Argyll' comes from the Gaelic *Earra-Ghaidheal* meaning the boundary or frontier land of the Gaels. It was indeed frontier territory, for the Gaels, a people of Celtic ethnicity who migrated from Ireland, inevitably found other peoples already established. Nevertheless, by about 500AD they were able to establish the kingdom of Dál Riata in Argyll. This name was taken from that which already applied to a kingdom based on present-day County Antrim in Northern Ireland. When the seat of kingship was moved to Dunadd at the southern end of Kilmartin Glen this hill fort became the most important place in their realm. Following Irish tradition, a footprint

4

Campbeltown, one of the largest towns in Argyll, viewed from across Campbeltown Loch. **5**
The tower of Lorne & Lowland Church is prominent on the right.

was carved in a flat rock on Dunadd's summit and the king was inaugurated by placing his foot into the imprint (see picture on p.1). There are few places in Scotland where one can engage so directly with Scotland's distant past. Kilmartin Glen is one of Scotland's richest archaeological landscapes, where there are over 350 archaeological and historical monuments within a six-mile radius. Many of these are of national and international importance and many more of regional significance. The surviving monuments go back to the Neolithic and Bronze Ages. The abundance of standing stones, burial cairns and carved stones have left us with an impressive legacy from these early times.

Celtic Christianity came to Scotland as a result of the missionary work of St Columba (521–597) and those who followed him. In 563 he landed on the southern tip of Kintyre where only about 12 miles of sea separate it from Ireland. The legacy of the early evangelists is still vivid in these parts.

To cover the ground in a reasonably logical

Campbeltown's mild climate enables palm trees to thrive here.

ay, this book begins at Campbeltown in the extreme south and works its way up Kintyre. It continues up the western seaboard before heading east to Inveraray, then returning to the west coast at Oban. Thereafter, the inland areas of Loch Awe, Glen Orchy and Loch Etive are explored, the journey ending where northern Argyll meets Lochaber, subject of another book in this series. The remaining, eastern, part of Argyll's mainland is covered in *Picturing Scotland: Loch Lomond, Cowal & Bute*. The islands of Mull and Iona also have their own volume in this series.

But now, let this photographic journey remind you of or prepare you for the best that this impressive land has to show. Whether your interest lies in trekking up mountains like Ben Cruachan or Ben Starav, soaking up the splendour of castles such as Kilchurn or Inveraray, delving into the misty past or stretching out on those fabulous beaches, let the exploration begin!

Campbeltown Picture House, one of Scotland's earliest purpose-built cinemas, opened its doors in May 1913. Today it is the oldest cinema in Scotland still showing films.

8   Dawn over Campbeltown Loch with Davaar Island in the centre. It can only be accessed at low tide via a mile-long causeway from the mainland. One good reason to visit the island is Archibald

MacKinnon's cave painting of the crucifixion, a work he did in secret in 1887, creating something of a mystery locally. MacKinnon, a local artist, claimed the painting in 1934.

10 This rocky outcrop, resembling a crouching lion, was the setting for Dunaverty Castle, a fortified site for over 1,000 years from around 500AD. It is near the village of Southend.

The final stage of the road to Mull of Kintyre lighthouse snakes dramatically down **11** a drop of 335m/1100ft. The lighthouse dates back to 1788.

12　Machrihanish, five miles west of Campbeltown, is noted for its fine beach and first-class golf course the popularity of which once kept a light railway from Campbeltown busy!

On the east coast of Kintyre, Kildonan Dun was probably built in the first or second century AD and 13 shares constructional similarities with the brochs found in north and north-west Scotland.

14 South of Carradale and situated overlooking the sea, construction of Torrisdale Castle began in 1815. It was extended in the early 20th century and today is run as an environmentally sustainable estate.

Carradale enjoys a fine location on Kintyre's east coast with views across to the Isle of Arran. **15**
This is Port Righ, a small settlement overlooking this lovely bay south of the main village.

16 An aerial view of Carradale harbour which remains an active fishing port. Visiting Carradale requires a short detour off the 'main' road through these parts and is well worth seeing.

Continuing up the east Kintyre coast, the tiny village of Grogport looks across Kilbrannan Sound to the Isle of Arran (see *Picturing Scotland: Arran & Ayrshire*).

18 Left: Skipness Castle in north-east Kintyre was begun in the early 13th century when Argyll was ruled not by Scotland but by Norway. Right: the 16th-century tower house at Skipness.

From the top of Skipness Castle's tower house, a view which gives an idea of its setting. **19**
In the field towards top left are the ruins of the 13th-century St Brendan's Chapel.

20 Over on the west side of Kintyre is Glenbarr Abbey which houses the Clan MacAlister Centre. It is open to the public from April to September. Clan MacAlister is an offshoot (sept) of Clan Donald.

Continuing up the western side of Kintyre there are miles of glorious beaches like this one at **21**
A'Chleit, south of the village of Tayinloan, from where a ferry crosses to the Isle of Gigha.

22 And over on Gigha ('God's Island'), these two views capture something of what there is to see at Achamore Gardens.

Gigha is a delightful little island. This is the exquisite little Ardminish Bay. The crowd on the beach **23** are enjoying some live music, part of the Gigha Music Festival.

24 This glorious panorama looks north from Kintyre over West Loch Tarbert and into Knapdale. The ferry on the right is berthed at the small port of Kennacraig from where it will sail to the

lands of Islay and Colonsay.

26 Looking from Kennacraig early on a beautiful summer morning, West Loch Tarbert stretches away towards Gigha.

Tarbert sits at the north end of Kintyre on the isthmus that attaches Kintyre to the rest of Argyll. **27**
It is an attractive town and harbour which can look as enchanting by night as by day.

28 It has been a place of shelter for at least a thousand years and its harbour remains busy today. The name 'Tarbert' means a narrow piece of land between two areas of water.

Tarbert Castle stands above the town, guarding the anchorage below in the bay and controlling **29** the narrow land link between East Loch Tarbert and West Loch Tarbert.

30 Lochgilphead stands at the head of Loch Gilp, a small loch on the west side of Loch Fyne. The town was first laid out as a planned settlement in about 1790 and is Argyll's administrative capital.

About three miles from Lochgilphead at Cairnbaan there are several sets of these 'cup-and-ring' **31** markings carved into natural stone slabs. Made about 5,000 years ago, their purpose is uncertain.

32 Beavers were released in Knapdale Forest during May 2009 and have settled in well to their new home. The first kits were born in August 2010, one of which is seen here with an adult beaver.

The Crinan Canal runs from Ardrishaig (near Lochgilphead) to Crinan. It is pictured here near **33** Belanoch in evening shadow which accentuates the brightness of the cloud reflection in the water.

34 The canal opened in 1801. It was built to provide a shortcut from the Clyde estuary to Hebridean waters. Crinan is at its western end where the canal meets the Sound of Jura.

Two to three thousand vessels, mostly pleasure craft, pass through the canal each year. **35**
The canal basin at Crinan always seems to be hosting some lovely old boats.

36 From Crinan we venture south into Knapdale to find the remote village of Tayvallich. It is a particularly well-sheltered haven, situated around a bay on the west side of Loch Sween.

On the opposite side of same loch and further south, Castle Sween is a contender for being the
oldest standing castle in Scotland, built by Sven The Red in the 12th century.

38 Now we move north into Kilmartin Glen (see introduction) and the Gaels' hill fort of Dunadd. This was once one of the most important places in (what became) Scotland.

From about 500 to 900 this 175ft-high outcrop was where the kings of Dál Riata were anointed. **39**
The picture shows part of the way to the summit, showing what a defensible place it was.

40 In the south of Knapdale is the 'island' of Danna, a very remote spot from where some spectacular views can be enjoyed. Taken towards the end of a severe winter, this long-range shot reaches the vas

...ountain wall of Ben Cruachan in northern Argyll, about 40 miles away.

42 The Kilmartin area is rich in ancient sites such as Temple Wood stone circles, the southern of which is above. They date back to at least 3,000BC, this one taking over from the earlier northern one.

There are several settings of standing stones in Kilmartin Glen. The shadows of the nearer stones **43** point the way to the others in this alignment which stretches across the field at Nether Largie.

44 Nearby is Nether Largie south cairn, the only chambered cairn of the five in Kilmartin's 2km-long linear cemetery. Excavations have revealed evidence of it being used for as much as a thousand yea

Left: carving on the rear of an early stone crucifix in Kilmartin Church. **45**
Right: reconstruction of a hermit's cell at the excellent Kilmartin House Museum.

46 Continuing north up Kilmartin Glen reveals 16th-century Carnasserie Castle (Historic Scotland) on the hillside to the west of the road. It was the residence of the first Protestant Bishop of the Isles

It is also where the first book to be printed in Gaelic was written. Above, this remnant arch at **47** Carnasserie look as much a part of the landscape as the trees which frame it.

48 The 'grain' of the land in Argyll has created a series of sea lochs which reach deep into the coastline as demonstrated here by Loch Craignish. The land on the far side is the Ardfern peninsula.

Right: seen here, from above Craobh Haven on the mainland are the tips of two islands, Shuna and Luing (upper right) while in the distance are Scarba (right) and Jura (left). Above: in the Gulf of Corryvreckan between Scarba and Jura, the combination of an underwater rock pinnacle and certain sea conditions produce turbulence that creates a whirlpool, or standing waves several feet high as in this picture.

49

50 Argyll's climate makes it ideal for many wonderful gardens. The National Trust for Scotland's Arduaine Garden is a particularly fine example. Situated on a promontory overlooking Loch Melfort,

Arduaine is best known for its spring rhododendron collection, yet is alive with flowers and fragrance throughout the season.

52 At the head of Loch Melfort near the village of Kilmelford, the colours and hillside textures seen here are typical of Argyll's landscape.

The island of Seil is separated from the mainland (far side of bridge) by the narrowest sliver of sea. **53**
But as this is an inlet of the ocean, it is romantically referred to as the 'Bridge over the Atlantic'.

54 On the west of Seil, at the foot of the cliff, is the village of Easdale. A little confusingly, the aerial view opposite is of the island of Easdale which lies just yards off Seil. Easdale and Seil were jointly

a major centre of the slate industry which led to them being known as the 'Islands that Roofed the World'. Several now-flooded quarries can be seen in the picture above.

56 We now interrupt our northerly progress and flit about 20 miles east to the beautiful town of Inveraray, a planned settlement built on the shores of Loch Fyne from 1743 to replace the original

llage that was demolished to make way for the castle. The picture was taken from Duniquaich st after dawn on an autumn day.

58 This is the view from Inveraray looking over to where the previous picture was taken, from close to the tower at the top of Duniquaich, the hill behind the twin-arch bridge.

Inveraray Castle is a remarkable and unique piece of architecture incorporating Baroque, **59** Palladian and Gothic styles. It took over 40 years to build, from 1746 to 1789.

60 Inveraray's location can be appreciated when seen from the top of The Duke's Tower. Looking north-east, the Arrochar Alps can be seen in the distance.

Inveraray Jail is the town's principal visitor attraction, offering an interactive experience of life in a **61** 19th-century prison. In the courtroom scene, the trial continues!

62 South-west of Inveraray is Auchindrain, a restored highland township. The conserved buildings have been furnished and equipped, presenting a fascinating glimpse into highland life in the past.

A few miles further on are Crarae Gardens, on the shores of Loch Fyne. Trees and shrubs from all over the temperate world thrive here (National Trust for Scotland). **63**

64 No pictorial study of Argyll would be complete without a view of Loch Lomond, the northern reaches of which are seen here from Beinn Dubh.

West of Loch Lomond are the Arrochar Alps. Ben Arthur, usually known as The Cobbler, **65** is their most distinctive mountain at 884m/2900ft. It stands above the village of Arrochar.

66 Returning to Argyll's west coast, Oban is its largest town and a major port for ferries to the Hebrides. In this evening scene, McCaig's Tower is floodlit and the Mull ferry is berthed for the night.

Evening shadows in McCaig's Tower, Oban. John Stuart McCaig built it during the winters of 1895 **67** to 1902 to provide work for stonemasons who were otherwise unemployed at that time of year.

68 Oban (meaning 'little bay' in Gaelic) is a popular resort that grew rapidly after the arrival of the railway from Glasgow, although it had a steamship connection from there since 1812.

McCaig's Tower is a good place from which to appreciate Oban's maritime setting. **69**
This image shows what lies to the left of the front cover picture, including Pulpit Hill.

70 Model of a Sunderland flying boat at Oban's War and Peace Museum. During the Second World War, a squadron of these impressive planes was based in Oban Bay.

The Sunderlands were maintained at a facility on the island of Kerrera, just across the water from **71** Oban, where the present-day marina is located, as shown above.

72 Sailing on the ferries to and from Oban provides a different way of seeing the town. In this view, Corran Esplanade with the prominent tower of St Columba's Cathedral is on the left, beyond which

The waterfront is lined with some of the town's many hotels. The red-brick chimney of Oban Distillery is also visible.

74 Ferry routes from Oban go to Kerrera, Mull, Colonsay, Coll, Tiree and the Outer Hebrides.
Here, *Clansman* passes Lismore South Lighthouse on an outward voyage.

No visit to Oban is complete without an exploration of lovely Glen Lonan to the east of the town. **75**
This pastoral scene, complete with mountain backdrop, sums it up.

76 A few miles north of Oban, Dunstaffnage Castle was built by 1275 on a huge rock overlooking the Firth of Lorn and provided the MacDougalls with a mighty stronghold (Historic Scotland).

Close to the castle, among the trees, is Dunstaffnage Chapel, built in the 13th century. The remains **77** of the paired windows in the chancel show a high standard of workmanship (Historic Scotland).

78 Venturing inland now, this view from the grounds of the Ardanaiseig Hotel scans the northern reaches of Loch Awe. At 41km/25miles, it is Scotland's longest inland loch.

A Loch Awe panorama from its eastern side not far from the village of Cladich, taking in Innis **79** Chonain (Conan's Island) while Beinn Eunaich (989m/3244ft) is the peak towards the left

80 Kilchurn Castle, built by Sir Colin Campbell of Glenorchy c.1550, stands at the north end of Loch Awe. Much enlarged in 1693, it incorporates the first purpose-built barracks in Scotland.

A hydro-electric plant has been built inside Ben Cruachan. The dam of its storage reservoir can be **81**
seen half-way up the flank of the mountain.

82 The route up Ben Cruachan looks down into the hydro-electric scheme's reservoir, centre of picture with Loch Awe beyond. The power station opened in 1966 and today has also become one of the

...rea's main tourist attractions, with tours of the 'Hollow Mountain' taking visitors through this ...nnel to see the turbines and other workings of the plant.

84 Ben Cruachan rises from the head of Loch Awe and gives hill walkers a tough climb. At 1126m/3694 it is Scotland's 31st-highest mountain. This is the eastward view along Cruachan's granite ridge

...wards Ben Diamh (998m/3274ft), while above we look north up Glen Etive towards the Glen Coe **85** ...ountains, a good many miles away.

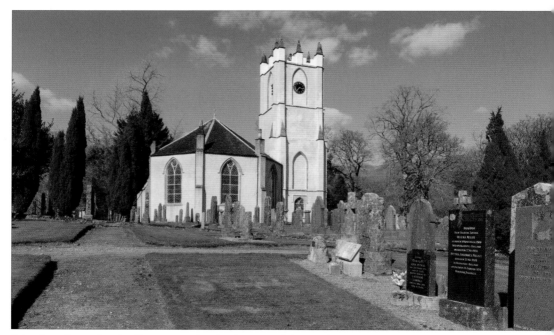

86 The village of Dalmally is a couple of miles east of the northern end of Loch Awe and is home to Glenorchy Church, built 1810-11 to an unusual octagonal design, with a tower on its eastern elevation.

Glen Orchy runs north-east from Dalmally, through which the picturesque River Orchy tumbles over **87** many waterfalls such as this one at Allt Broighleachan, a site of special scientific interest (SSSI).

88 The River Orchy flows out of beautiful Loch Tulla in the north-eastern corner of Argyll. The West Highland Way passes through this area, winding round the western end of the loch before crossing

the Black Mount (the hills in the distance) before entering Lochaber en route to Fort William.

90 The village of Bridge of Orchy is a mile or two south of Loch Tulla, on the road and rail routes to the north. The shadowed hill above the bridge is Beinn an Dothaidh, 1004m/3293ft.

Beinn an Dothaidh's neighbour, the beautifully conical Beinn Dorain (1076m/3530ft), **91**
greets the eye. The level line at its base is the Glasgow to Fort William/Mallaig railway.

92 Located near Taynuilt on the southern shore of Loch Etive, Bonawe Iron Furnace is the most complete charcoal-fuelled ironworks in Britain – a fascinating place to visit (Historic Scotland).

To the west of Bonawe, between Taynuilt and Connel on the southern shores of Loch Etive, **93**
is the beautiful Achnacloich Garden with its lovely spring colours.

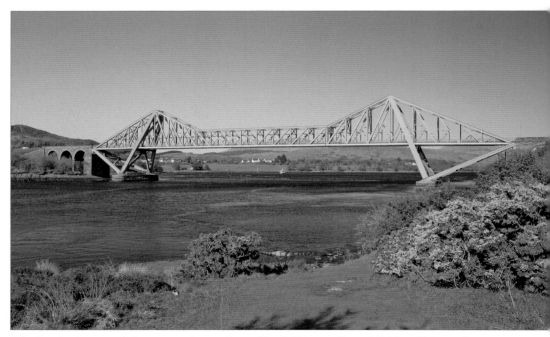

94 Continuing west brings us to the outflow of Loch Etive at Connel Bridge. This used to serve both road and rail but the railway branch line from Connel to Ballachulish closed in the 1960s.

Looking inland (east) from Connel Bridge reveals a point of interest that comes and goes: at high tide the water is calm but at low tide the Falls of Lora appear as the sea recedes.

96 These otters conjure up a lovely conversation: 'No, dear, I'll deal with this!' – and a baby seal at the Sea Life Sanctuary, near Barcaldine, Loch Creran, a few miles north of Connel.

Further on, the coastal main road (A828) crosses Loch Creran (a sea loch), from where this easterly **97** view captures Ben Sgulaird (937m/3073ft) in the distance.

98 A spring view of the village of Port Appin, from where the passenger ferry to the island of Lismore takes about five minutes. Lismore's north lighthouse can be seen in the distance.

A touch of afterglow under-lights the clouds in this evening view from Port Appin towards Lismore. **99**
About nine miles long, narrow, low-lying and fertile, it has a population of about 180.

100 Castle Stalker stands on an islet on the edge of Loch Linnhe near the village of Portnacroish. It dates back to the 15th century and was the traditional stronghold of the Stewarts of Appin.

From near Castle Stalker, this view looks across Loch Linnhe to the northern end of Lismore with **101** the heights of Morvern, a district of Lochaber, beyond. Oh, to be on that yacht!

102 Returning to Loch Etive for the last leg of the journey, the remains of Ardchattan Priory are located near the scene on pages 104-105. It was founded by the strict Valliscaulian order in 1231.

Rowan trees at Ardchattan. Their berries appear in August or September. Legend has it that the **103** rowan wards off evil spirits, which is why they were often planted at sacred sites.

104 A tranquil scene at the southern end of Loch Etive near Ardchattan, in the Benderloch district of Argyll. Just visible in the far distance is Dun da Ghaoithe on the island of Mull.

106 From the southern slopes of the Glen Coe mountains, a view into upper Glen Etive with Ben Starav (1078m/3536ft) rising dramatically from the valley floor.

The head of Loch Etive. From here it is 17 miles to the loch's outflow to the sea at Connel. **107**
Ben Cruachan can be seen in the distance . . .

108 . . . and when studied in close-up, the fearsome aspect of its summit ridge can be seen to good effect. For comparison, refer back to the picture of the ridge on page 84.

A perfect moment makes for a satisfying picture in Glen Etive. The peak towards the left in the distance is Glas Bheinn Mhor (997m/3270ft) and Ben Starav is on the right.

110 Glen Etive is a great place for lovers of waterfalls and rapids. In truth we are now pushing the definition of Argyll: it used to extend up to the south side of Glen Coe, but today belongs to

ochaber District of Highland Region. And speaking of Lochaber, our final view is a 'taster' of what
o expect there, with Buachaille Etive Beag and Buachaille Etive Mor reflected in a Glen Etive lochan.

Published 2018 by Lyrical Scotland, an imprint of Lomond Books Ltd, Broxburn, EH52 5NF
www.lyricalscotland.com www.lomondbooks.com

Originated by Ness Publishing, 47 Academy Street, Elgin, Moray, IV30 1LR
(First published by Ness Publishing 2015)

Printed in China

All photographs © Colin and Eithne Nutt except pp.12 & 49 (right) © Scotavia Images; pp.16 & 55 © Guthrie Aerial
Photography; p.32 © Steve Gardner/SWT; p.49 (left) © David Philip (hebridean-wild.co.uk); p.61 © Inveraray Jail;
p.83 © Cruachan Visitor Centre, ScottishPower; p.91 © Ian Evans/Mountain Images; p.96 (both) © Oban Sea Life Cent

Text © Colin Nutt
ISBN 978-1-78818-023-8

Front cover: Oban Bay; p.1: King's footprint, Dunadd; p.4: in Inveraray; this page: fishing boat, West Loch Tarbert;
back cover: Loch Etive and Ben Cruachan